DATE DUE

IMMANUEL LUTHERAN LIBRARY

floor exercise
and
vaulting

Consultant

Kathleen Shelly, Assistant Professor
Women's Physical Education
Sacramento State College
Sacramento, California

Demonstrator

Barbara Parcher
Sacramento State College

IMMANUEL LUTHERAN LIBRARY

published by:
The Athletic Institute
Merchandise Mart, Chicago

*A not-for-profit organization
devoted to the advancement of
athletics, physical education
and recreation.*

Robert G. Bluth, Editor

© The Athletic Institute 1973
All Rights Reserved

**Library of Congress
Catalog Card Number 79-109498**

**"Sports Techniques" Series
SBN 87670-080-6**

**Published by The Athletic Institute
Chicago, Illinois 60654**

Foreword

The SPORTS TECHNIQUES SERIES is but one item in a comprehensive list of sports instructional aids which are made available by The Athletic Institute. This book is part of a master plan which seeks to make the benefits of athletics, physical education and recreation available to everyone.

The Athletic Institute is a not-for-profit organization devoted to the advancement of athletics, physical education and recreation. The Institute believes that participation in athletics and recreation has benefits of inestimable value to the individual and to the community.

The nature and scope of the many Institute programs are determined by a *Professional Advisory Committee,* whose members are noted for their outstanding knowledge, experience and ability in the fields of athletics, physical education and recreation.

The Institute believes that through this book the reader will become a better performer, skilled in the fundamentals of this fine event. Knowledge and the practice necessary to mold knowledge into playing ability are the keys to real enjoyment in playing any game or sport.

Gymnastics aids in the development of motor skills, flexibility, agility and endurance as well as providing enjoyable recreation.

Donald E. Bushore
Executive Director
The Athletic Institute

Introduction

The floor exercise and vaulting movements are presented using beginning and intermediate skills. It is impossible to show every move of these levels in these few pages.

Each skill is presented with the intention that it be used as a basic or leadup skill, with good control and form so that the gymnast may progress to more advanced skills and eventually on to floor exercise creative work.

As soon as the gymnast has acquired the ability to perform a particular movement, she should be encouraged to put it with another one so as to begin developing a routine. Ultimately, the routine becomes the full expression of a floor exercise.

Kathy Shelly

Table of Contents

Table of Contents (Continued)

poses

Poses are momentarily held positions which are used to accent a musical phrase or to attract the judges' attention to a particular part of the exercise.

Kneeling Arch

Start in a kneeling position with arms at your side and head in a normal position.

Drop your head backward. Arch backward from a low back. Arms are held obliquely downward with palms in.

End in a kneeling arch position with your thighs and hips at a right angle to the lower legs. Low back is arched. Head is back. Arms are extended downward in an oblique.

1. KNEEL WITH ARMS AT SIDE AND HEAD STRAIGHT.
2. DROP HEAD BACKWARD. ARCH BACKWARD FROM LOW BACK. ARMS ARE OBLIQUELY DOWNWARD WITH PALMS UP.
3. END IN KNEELING ARCH POSITION WITH THIGHS AND HIPS AT RIGHT ANGLE TO LOWER LEGS. LOW BACK IS ARCHED; HEAD IS BACK; ARMS ARE DOWNWARD OBLIQUE.

Inverted Back Scale

Start in a stand on your left leg with the right foot pointed in front. Arms are obliquely downward in front. Head is in a normal position.

Lift your right leg in front. Push the left hip forward and arch in low back. Tuck chin to chest to maintain balance while leaning back. Arms are at your sides, with palms facing up.

Lean back and rotate your arms down and backward to position them overhead with palms facing out. Drop head back. Lift your right leg to a split position.

End momentarily in a balance on the straight left leg. Right leg lifts in front to split. Upper body is downward with arms overhead.

1. STAND ON LEFT LEG—RIGHT FOOT POINTED IN FRONT, ARMS OBLIQUELY DOWN IN FRONT, HEAD STRAIGHT.
2. LIFT RIGHT LEG IN FRONT.
3. PUSH LEFT HIP FORWARD; ARCH LOW BACK.
4. KEEP CHIN TUCKED TO CHEST TO MAINTAIN BALANCE WHILE LEANING BACK. ARMS ARE AT SIDES AND PALMS FACE UPWARD.
5. LEAN BACK. ROTATE ARMS DOWN AND BACKWARD TO POSITION OVERHEAD. PALMS FACE OUT.
6. DROP HEAD BACK.
7. LIFT RIGHT LEG UP TO SPLIT POSITION.
8. END IN MOMENTARY BALANCE ON STRAIGHT LEFT LEG. LIFT RIGHT LEG IN FRONT TO SPLIT POSITION. UPPER BODY EXTENDS DOWNWARD. ARMS ARE OVERHEAD.

Lunge

Start in a stand on the turned-out left leg with the right foot pointed in front.

Kick a straight right leg upward and forward. Land on a bent right leg with your weight shifted to the center.

Arch backward and drop your head back. Arms are curved with the left arm extended horizontally. Palms face in.

End in a lunge position (pose) with the right leg bent and left leg turned out straight. Back is arched and head is back. Arms are curved horizontally to floor—left in front, right by right ear.

1. START BY STANDING ON TURNED-OUT LEFT LEG. RIGHT FOOT POINTS IN FRONT.
2. KICK STRAIGHT RIGHT LEG UP AND FORWARD. LAND ON BENT RIGHT LEG. SHIFT WEIGHT TO CENTER.
3. ARCH BACKWARD. DROP HEAD BACK. ARMS CURVED—LEFT IS HORIZONTAL IN FRONT; RIGHT IS HORIZONTAL IN BACK. PALMS ARE IN.
4. END IN LUNGE POSITION—RIGHT LEG BENT; LEFT LEG TURNED OUT STRAIGHT BEHIND. BACK IS ARCHED AND HEAD IS BACK. ARMS CURVED HORIZONTALLY TO FLOOR—LEFT ARM IN FRONT AND RIGHT ARM BY RIGHT EAR.

Lunge, Arms Crossed

Start in a stand on a turned-out left leg with your right foot pointed in front.

Kick the straight right leg up and forward. Land on the bent right leg with your weight shifted to the center.

Arch backward and drop your head back. Arms are crossed, elbow to elbow, with the right hand on left shoulder and the left hand on the right shoulder. Left arm is closest to body. Elbows point upward.

End in a lunge position with the right leg bent and the left leg turned out and straight. Back is arched. Head is back. Elbows point up with arms crossed and hands on opposite shoulders. Left arm is inside right arm.

1. START BY STANDING ON TURNED OUT LEFT LEG. RIGHT FOOT POINTED IN FRONT.
2. KICK STRAIGHT RIGHT LEG UP AND FORWARD. LAND ON BENT LEG AND SHIFT WEIGHT TO CENTER.
3. ARCH BACKWARD, DROP HEAD BACK. ARMS CROSSED ELBOW TO ELBOW—RIGHT HAND ON LEFT SHOULDER; LEFT HAND ON RIGHT SHOULDER. LEFT ARM IS NEAREST BODY. ELBOWS POINT UPWARD.
4. END IN LUNGE POSITION—RIGHT LEG BENT AND LEFT LEG TURNED OUT STRAIGHT. BACK IS ARCHED AND HEAD IS BACK. ELBOWS POINT UP. ARMS ARE CROSSED WITH HANDS ON OPPOSITE SHOULDERS (LEFT ARM NEAREST BODY).

10

jumps and leaps

Jumps and leaps are used to accentuate a dynamic part of the routine or to make transitions. If of adequate difficulty, they may provide part of the difficulties required in a floor exercise routine.

Tuck Jump, Legs Back

Stand with feet together, arms back and head in a normal position.

Bend knees and ankles while keeping your back straight.

Jump up, extending the knees and pushing off your toes. Swing your arms forward to an oblique horizontal with palms up.

At the height of the jump, bend knees and heels toward your buttocks. Look up to the left with your head.

Pause in air with knees bent and heels toward buttocks. Arms are obliquely forward at the horizontal with palms up. Head is also up and to the left. Land on two feet. Bend the knees to absorb the force of landing.

1. **STAND WITH FEET TOGETHER, ARMS BACKWARD AND HEAD IN NORMAL POSITION.**
2. **BEND KNEES AND ANKLES; KEEP BACK STRAIGHT.**
3. **JUMP UP, PUSHING OFF TOES AND EXTENDING KNEES. SWING ARMS FORWARD TO OBLIQUE HORIZONTAL. PALMS ARE UP.**
4. **BEND KNEES AT HEIGHT OF JUMP AND BRING HEELS TOWARD BUTTOCKS. HEAD LOOKS UP TO LEFT.**
5. **PAUSE IN AIR WITH KNEES BENT AND HEELS UP IN BACK. ARMS ARE HELD OBLIQUELY FORWARD AT HORIZONTAL. PALMS ARE UP.**
6. **LAND ON TWO FEET. BEND KNEES TO ABSORB FORCE ON LANDING.**

Arch Jump, Legs Split

Start in stand with your right foot in front of the left. Arms are crossed at the forearms. Left arm is nearest body with palms in.

Bend at the hips, knees and ankles. Keep your back straight.

Push hard off your feet and toes to jump upward. Thrust the arms out and upward with palms turning out.

Kick your left leg up and back to a split position. Bend your knee to bring the left foot over your forehead. Right leg is straight, head is back and your back is arched.

Pause in the air with a straight right leg pointed downward. A bent left leg is up in back with foot overhead. Arms are obliquely positioned overhead with palms out. Back is arched and head is back.

Land on your right leg with the left leg behind. Bend your knees to absorb the force. This is a quick forceful jump.

1. **START IN STAND WITH RIGHT FOOT IN FRONT OF LEFT AND ARMS CROSSED AT FOREARMS.**
2. **PUSH HARD OFF FEET AND TOES. THRUST ARMS OUT AND UP WHILE KICKING LEFT LEG UP IN BACK TO SPLIT POSITION.**
3. **PAUSE IN AIR WITH STRAIGHT RIGHT LEG POINTED DOWNWARD. LAND ON RIGHT LEG WITH LEFT LEG BEHIND.**

Stag Leap

Start from a walk or run of a few steps. Step onto the left leg. Bend the knee. Right arm is down in front, left arm obliquely backward.

Kick your right leg forward and up. Push up off of the left leg and swing your arms forward and upward. At the height of the leap, bend the right knee and pull your foot back toward the left leg.

Pause in the air. Legs are split with right knee bent and left leg parallel to the mat in back. Head is up, looking over your right arm.

Right arm is above left arm in forward oblique position. Land on the right leg with the left leg up in back. Bend your right knee to absorb the shock.

1. START FROM WALK OR RUN OF A FEW STEPS.
2. STEP ONTO LEFT LEG AND BEND KNEE. RIGHT ARM IS DOWN IN FRONT, LEFT ARM OBLIQUELY BACKWARD.
3. KICK RIGHT LEG FORWARD AND UP. PUSH UP OFF LEFT LEG; SWING ARMS FORWARD AND UP.
4. AT HEIGHT OF LEAP, BEND RIGHT KNEE. PULL FOOT BACK TOWARD LEFT LEG.
5. PAUSE IN AIR. LEGS SPLIT WITH RIGHT KNEE BENT. LEFT LEG IS BACK, PARALLEL TO MAT, WITH HEAD UP LOOKING OVER LEFT ARM.
6. LAND ON RIGHT LEG. LEFT LEG IS UP IN BACK. FOR CONTROL, BEND RIGHT KNEE TO ABSORB FORCE OF LANDING.

Stride or Split Leap

Start from a walk or run of a few steps with arms swinging at your sides

Step onto the left leg. Kick a straight right leg up and forward to the horizontal. Push off your left foot. Pull the left leg up in back to the horizontal. Arms swing forward and upward to help lift body.

At the height of the leap, the legs are split with your right leg in front. Knees are tight and straight, toes are pointed and head is up. Arms are up in a forward oblique with the right arm higher than the left. Palms face out. All body parts pause momentarily in the air.

Land on your right leg. Bend your knee to maintain control and absorb the force of landing. Left leg is straight and held tightly behind. Head is up with arms obliquely forward, the right higher than the left.

1. START FROM WALK OR RUN OF A FEW STEPS WITH ARMS SWINGING AT SIDES.
2. STEP ONTO LEFT LEG. KICK STRAIGHT RIGHT LEG UP AND FORWARD TO HORIZONTAL.
3. PUSH OFF LEFT FOOT. PULL LEFT LEG UP IN BACK TO HORIZONTAL. ARMS ARE FORWARD AND UPWARD TO HELP LIFT BODY.
4. AT HEIGHT OF LEAP, LEGS ARE SPLIT—RIGHT LEG IN FRONT WITH KNEES TIGHT AND STRAIGHT. TOES ARE POINTED, HEAD IS UP, ARMS ARE OBLIQUELY FORWARD WITH RIGHT ARM HIGHER THAN LEFT. PALMS FACE OUT. ALL BODY PARTS PAUSE MOMENTARILY.
5. LAND ON RIGHT LEG. BEND KNEE TO MAINTAIN CONTROL AND ABSORB FORCE. LEFT LEG IS STRAIGHT AND TIGHT IN BACK. HEAD IS UP. ARMS ARE OBLIQUELY FORWARD WITH RIGHT ARM HIGHER THAN LEFT.

floor movements

Back Shoulder Roll to Chest Roll Down

Start in a sit position with legs together and straight out in front of the body. Arms are out to your sides. Lean backward, tucking chin to chest. Lift legs as you start to roll on your back.

Roll onto the shoulders. Hips are piked. Arms and palms are on the mat. Left ear is toward left shoulder.

Thrust legs upward to open hips. Press hard against your hands. Roll over the right shoulder with your head directed to the left. Pull your head through as your body shoots upward. Turn the hands over. Squeeze your legs tightly together. Press against hands and keep your back arched to control the leg's coming down.

Roll from chest to stomach, then to the front of your hips, and finally to your thighs. Keep the back tight.

End in an arched position on the thighs with legs straight and toes pointed. Arms are straight with fingers pointed forward. Chin is lifted.

1. **START IN SIT WITH LEGS TOGETHER AND STRAIGHT OUT IN FRONT OF BODY. ARMS ARE OUT TO SIDES.**
2. **LEAN BACK; TUCK CHIN TO CHEST. LIFT LEGS AS YOU START TO ROLL BACK.**
3. **ROLL ONTO SHOULDERS WITH HIPS PIKED AND ARMS AND PALMS ON MAT.**

4. THRUST LEGS UPWARD TO OPEN HIPS. PRESS HARD AGAINST HANDS.
5. ROLL OVER RIGHT SHOULDER; HEAD IS TO LEFT. PULL HEAD THROUGH AS BODY SHOOTS UPWARD. TURN HANDS OVER.
6. SQUEEZE LEGS TIGHTLY TOGETHER. PRESS AGAINST HAND, KEEPING BACK ARCHED TO CONTROL LEGS' COMING DOWN.

7. ROLL DOWN FROM CHEST, TO STOMACH, THEN TO FRONT OF HIPS, AND FINALLY TO THIGHS. KEEP BACK TIGHT.
8. END IN ARCHED POSITION ON THIGHS WITH LEGS STRAIGHT. TOES ARE POINTED, ARMS, STRAIGHT AND FINGERS POINTED FORWARD. CHIN IS LIFTED.

IMMANUEL LUTHERAN LIBRARY

Sit Spin

Start in a tucked sit with knees together and right leg crossed over left at the ankle. Left arm is held horizontally in front. Right hand is on the mat, with fingers pointing away from your body. Body leans back onto the right arm while toes point off the mat.

Pull your body toward the right arm to initiate a spin to the right on your buttocks. Right arm swings to a curved position by your right ear. Head faces downward. Left arm is curved in front of your knees.

End in a tucked sit with knees together. Right arm curves overhead and left arm is in front of knees. Right leg crosses over left at the ankles. Toes are pointed with head facing forward to complete a full turn.

1. **START IN TUCKED SIT WITH KNEES TOGETHER AND RIGHT LEG CROSSED OVER LEFT AT ANKLE. LEFT ARM HELD HORIZONTALLY IN FRONT. RIGHT HAND IS ON MAT WITH FINGERS POINTING AWAY FROM BODY. BODY LEANS BACK ON RIGHT ARM. TOES POINT OFF MAT.**

2. **PULL BODY TOWARD RIGHT ARM TO INITIATE RIGHT SPIN ON BUTTOCKS.**
3. **RIGHT ARM SWINGS TO CURVED POSITION BY RIGHT EAR. LEFT ARM CURVED IN FRONT OF KNEES AND HEAD IS DOWN.**
4. **END IN TUCKED SIT—KNEES TOGETHER, RIGHT LEG CROSSED OVER LEFT AT ANKLES, TOES POINTED. ARMS ARE CURVED, WITH THE RIGHT OVERHEAD AND THE LEFT IN FRONT OF KNEES. HEAD IS DIRECTED FORWARD COMPLETING FULL TURN FORWARD.**

Straddle Spin on Back (Russian Turn)

Start in a split position with your right leg in front and left leg in back. Your right hand is on mat beside the right leg. Body leans back. Now the right hand is on mat beside the right leg. Lean your body forward. Left arm is held obliquely backward with palm pointing down.

Swing your left arm backward. Follow the arm to the left with your body pushing off the right arm.

Swing the right leg to the left and close to the mat. Put your left hand on mat, bend arm at the elbow. Cross the right leg over close to the left leg. Lean back against the mat.

Push with your right hand and pull with the left arm to start a spin while entirely on your back. Right leg continues a flat circle to the left.

When your legs reach a straddle position, spin the shoulders on the mat with hips up.

At end of a full spin, pull your legs together in a tight pike position. Make one half-turn more and roll forward. Bend your left leg under the right.

End in sit with the left shin on mat and tucked under the bent right leg. Right toes point on the mat, back is straight and arms are obliquely downward in back. Hold your head in a normal position.

1. **START IN SPLIT—RIGHT LEG IN FRONT, LEFT LEG IN BACK, RIGHT HAND ON MAT BESIDE RIGHT LEG. BODY LEANS FORWARD. LEFT ARM IS OBLIQUELY BACKWARD WITH PALM DOWN.**

2. SWING LEFT ARM BACKWARD. FOLLOW ARM WITH BODY, PUSH OFF RIGHT ARM.
3. SWING RIGHT LEG TO LEFT, CLOSE TO MAT. PLACE BENT LEFT ARM ON MAT.
4. CROSS RIGHT LEG CLOSELY OVER LEFT LEG.
5. LEAN BACK AGAINST MAT.
6. PUSH WITH RIGHT HAND AND PULL WITH LEFT ARM TO START SPIN WHILE ENTIRELY ON BACK. RIGHT LEG CONTINUES IN A FLAT CIRCLE TO THE LEFT.
7. SPIN ON SHOULDERS WITH HIPS UP WHEN LEGS REACH STRADDLE POSITION.
8. AT END OF FULL SPIN, PULL LEGS TOGETHER IN TIGHT PIKE.
9. MAKE ONE HALF-TURN MORE.
10. ROLL FORWARD; BEND LEFT LEG UNDER RIGHT LEG.
11. END IN SIT WITH LEFT SHIN ON MAT AND TUCKED UNDER BENT RIGHT LEG. TOES ARE POINTED ON MAT, BACK IS STRAIGHT, ARMS ARE OBLIQUELY DOWN IN BACK. HEAD IS IN NORMAL POSITION.
12. THIS IS A ONE- AND ONE-HALF TURN.

turns

Turns are usually used as transitions between movements or as a means of changing direction.

Chainé Turn

Start in a side stand with your weight on the balls of your feet. Arms are slightly curved at the side horizontal. Head focuses on a point over the right shoulder.

Shift your weight to the right foot. Turn your body one half-turn to the right. Swing the left foot in front of the right to put it at the side of the right leg to complete the half-turn. Snap your head around quickly to the right. Bring the right leg around with the body to put your foot down at side of the left leg.

End in same position as you started, having made a half-turn on each step.

1. **START IN SIDE STAND WITH WEIGHT ON BALLS OF FEET AND ARMS CURVED AT SIDE HORIZONTAL. HEAD DIRECTED OVER RIGHT SHOULDER.**
2. **SHIFT WEIGHT TO RIGHT FOOT. TURN BODY ONE HALF-TURN TO RIGHT. SWING LEFT LEG IN FRONT OF RIGHT, AND STEP ON LEFT FOOT TO SIDE.**
3. **SHIFT WEIGHT TO LEFT LEG AND CONTINUE TO TURN RIGHT.**
4. **BRING RIGHT LEG AROUND WITH BODY TO PUT FOOT DOWN BESIDE LEFT LEG.**
5. **END IN START POSITION HAVING MADE A HALF-TURN ON EACH STEP.**

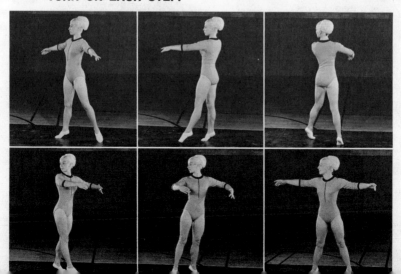

Tour Jeté (leap with turn)

Start from a step or a slide. Arms are in a low oblique backward.

Step onto the left leg. Kick your right leg up and forward. Rise onto the ball of the left foot. Swing your arms up to the vertical. Pivot three-eighths of a turn to the left on the left foot.

Look to the left with the head and turn your body one-eighth of a circle to push off the left foot. Scissor your legs in the air so that the left leg changes position with the right leg. Split your legs with a straight right leg extending downward and the left leg up in back.

Land on the right leg, bending it to absorb force of landing. Hold up your left leg in back and arms up by front of your face.

End in a lunge with the right leg bent in front and a straight left leg turned out behind. Also, back is straight and arms are curved in front of your face to complete a half turn.

1. **START FROM STEP OR SLIDE. ARMS ARE LOW IN AN OBLIQUE BACKWARD.**
2. **STEP ONTO LEFT LEG.**

3. KICK RIGHT LEG UP AND FORWARD. RISE ONTO BALL OF LEFT FOOT.
4. SWING ARMS TO VERTICAL. PIVOT THREE-EIGHTHS OF TURN TO LEFT.
5. LOOK TO LEFT. TURN BODY ONE-EIGHTH OF A CIRCLE. PUSH OFF LEFT FOOT.
6. SCISSOR LEGS IN AIR BEHIND BODY. LEGS REVERSE POSITIONS. SPLIT LEGS WITH STRAIGHT RIGHT LEG EXTENDED DOWNWARD. LEFT LEG IS UP IN BACK.
7. LAND ON RIGHT LEG. BEND KNEE TO ABSORB FORCE. LEFT LEG IS HELD UP IN BACK. ARMS ARE UP BY FRONT OF FACE.
8. END IN LUNGE POSITION WITH RIGHT LEG BENT IN FRONT. STRAIGHT LEFT LEG IS TURNED OUT BEHIND. BACK IS STRAIGHT AND ARMS ARE CURVED IN FRONT OF FACE TO COMPLETE A HALF-TURN.

Full Turn in Back Attitude Position

Start in a side stand on the straight left leg with the right leg pointed to the side. Left arm is held horizontally in back. Right arm is curved in front of the chest as your head faces over the right shoulder.

Step onto the right leg, bending it slightly at the knee. Swing the right arm across and out to the right side, then rise onto the ball of the right foot.

Lift your left leg up while bending to a back-attitude position. Knee is bent; thigh and lower leg are parallel to the mat.

Pivot a full turn on the ball of the right foot. Your right arm leads the turn. End in a stand on the right leg with the left leg in a back attitude. Right arm is obliquely backward. Left arm is held horizontally in front of the body with your head up.

1. START IN SIDE STAND ON STRAIGHT LEFT LEG. RIGHT LEG POINTS TO SIDE—LEFT LEG IS HORIZONTAL IN BACK, RIGHT ARM CURVES IN FRONT OF CHEST AND HEAD FACES OVER RIGHT SHOULDER.

2. STEP ONTO RIGHT LEG. BEND LEG.
3. SWING RIGHT ARM ACROSS AND OUT TO RIGHT SIDE.
4. RISE ONTO BALL OF RIGHT FOOT.
5. LIFT LEFT LEG UP BEHIND, TO BACK ATTITUDE POSITION—KNEE BENT, THIGH AND LOWER LEG PARALLEL TO MAT.
6. PIVOT FULL TURN TO RIGHT ON BALL OF FOOT (RIGHT). RIGHT ARM LEADS TURN.
7. END IN STAND ON RIGHT LEG. LEFT LEG IS IN BACK ATTITUDE. RIGHT ARM IS HELD OBLIQUELY BACKWARD. LEFT ARM IS HELD HORIZONTALLY IN FRONT WITH HEAD UP.

locomotor patterns

Locomotor patterns are used to cover the area and to help vary the floor pattern as well as to provide a change of pace by showing an unbroken phase.

Walk in Curved Pattern with Arm Push

Start in a stand on the balls of your feet. Twist your body to the left. Arms are crossed at the chest, left arm inside the right. Palms face outward. Step onto the right leg extending your left leg behind. Start arms pushing outward. Step onto the right foot as your body moves to the right and as your arms open further. Then step onto your left foot with your arms open.

Move onto the ball of the right foot. Left leg is lifted behind to the horizontal. Arms extend horizontally at your sides with palms backward. Head is up.

1. START IN STAND ON BALLS OF FEET WITH BODY TWISTED TO LEFT, ARMS CROSSED AT CHEST (LEFT ARM NEAREST BODY) AND PALMS EXTENDED OUT.
2. STEP ONTO LEFT LEG. EXTEND RIGHT LEG BEHIND AND START ARMS PUSHING OUTWARD.
3. STEP ONTO RIGHT FOOT. BODY MOVES TO RIGHT AS ARMS OPEN FURTHER.
4. STEP ONTO LEFT FOOT WITH ARMS OPEN.
5. MOVE ONTO BALL OF RIGHT FOOT. LEFT LEG LIFTS HORIZONTALLY BEHIND. ARMS ARE HELD HORIZONTALLY AT SIDE—PALMS BACK AND HEAD UP. STEPS SLANT TO RIGHT.

Low Walk to Arabesque

Start in a stand on both feet. Knees are bent and back is rounded with head down. Right arm curves downward in front. Left arm is held obliquely backward.

Step onto left leg (bent at knee). Lift your right arm by leading with the elbow and back of the wrist. Step onto the slightly bent right leg. Open the body as the right arm continues upward and left arm lowers in back.

Step onto an almost straight left leg. Right arm finishes with an oblique.

1. START IN STAND ON BOTH FEET—KNEES BENT, BACK ROUNDED, HEAD DOWN. RIGHT ARM CURVES DOWN IN FRONT. LEFT ARM IS HELD OBLIQUELY BACKWARD.
2. STEP ONTO BENT LEFT LEG. LIFT RIGHT ARM, LEAD WITH ELBOW AND BACK OF WRIST.
3. STEP ONTO SLIGHTLY BENT RIGHT LEG.
4. OPEN BODY AS RIGHT ARM CONTINUES UPWARD. LEFT ARM LOWERS IN BACK.
5. STEP ONTO AN ALMOST STRAIGHT LEFT LEG. RIGHT ARM FINISHES IN AN OBLIQUE LINE WITH THE LEFT ARM. HEAD IS UP.
6. STEP ONTO BALL OF FOOT (STRAIGHT RIGHT LEG). LIFT LEFT LEG IN BACK. LEFT ARM IS IN LINE WITH LEFT LEG. RIGHT ARM IS HELD VERTICALLY. HEAD IS UP.

Skip

Stand on the left leg with the right leg pointed in front. Arms are down at the sides.

Step onto the right leg. Swing the left leg forward and upward bending the knee. Push off the right foot (hop), extending the toes downward.

The right arm swings forward to the horizontal in front of the body as the left leg lifts forward. The left arm swings backward at the same time as the right arm swings forward. The arms move opposite to the legs.

This movement is done with an uneven rhythm.

1. **STAND ON LEFT LEG, RIGHT LEG POINTED IN FRONT. ARMS AT SIDES.**
2. **STEP FORWARD ONTO RIGHT LEG.**
3. **SWING LEFT LEG FORWARD AND UPWARD TO FRONT HORIZONTAL. BEND KNEE.**
4. **PUSH OFF RIGHT FOOT AND HOP, EXTENDING TOES TOWARD FLOOR.**
5. **SWING RIGHT ARM FORWARD TO FRONT HORIZONTAL AS LEFT LEG SWINGS FORWARD.**
6. **SWING LEFT ARM BACKWARD AS RIGHT ARM SWINGS FORWARD.**
7. **ARMS ARE OPPOSITE TO LEGS.**
8. **THIS MOVEMENT DONE WITH UNEVEN RHYTHM AND MAY BE REPEATED ON OTHER SIDE.**

stunts

Stunts are usually the means of obtaining the required number of difficulties in a routine. They should be logically spaced and should be of various degrees in difficulty. These are springy or power movements.

Forward Roll

Start in a squat position. Bend forward and place your hands on the mat, slightly ahead of the shoulders.

Take the weight on the arms. Lift hips upward by straightening your legs. Keep feet in contact with the mat.

Tuck chin to chest. Roll forward pushing off your feet. Keep the thighs close to your body with the back rounded. Bend the right knee as you roll onto the buttocks. Keep left leg straight extending your arms forward.

End in a sitting position with your arms forward. The right leg is bent and the left leg is straight.

Backward Roll

Start in a tucked sit with your feet on the mat and your arms forward. Lean the upper body back keeping your back rounded. Elbows are bent with hands near the ears and back of hands toward the shoulders. Chin is tucked to the chest.

As the body rolls backward to the shoulders, your hands contact the mat. The hips are off the mat and the knees are bent with thighs close to the chest.

Extend the toes toward the mat and over your head. Keep the hips low. When your feet are on mat, push hard with the arms to clear the head from the mat. End in a squat position with your arms forward.

1. START IN SQUAT POSITION.
2. BEND FORWARD. PLACE HANDS ON MAT IN FRONT OF SHOULDERS.
3. TAKE WEIGHT ON ARMS. LIFT HIPS BY STRAIGHTENING LEGS. KEEP FEET ON MAT.
4. TUCK CHIN. ROLL FORWARD BY PUSHING OFF FEET. ROUND BACK WITH THIGHS CLOSE TO BODY.
5. ROLL ONTO BUTTOCKS, BENDING RIGHT KNEE, AND KEEP LEFT LEG STRAIGHT. REACH ARMS FORWARD.
6. END IN A SIT WITH ARMS IN FRONT, RIGHT LEG BENT AND LEFT LEG STRAIGHT.

1. START IN TUCKED SIT. FEET ON MAT. ARMS FORWARD.
2. LEAN UPPER BODY BACK. KEEP BACK ROUNDED. ELBOWS BENT AND HANDS NEAR EARS. BACK OF HANDS ARE TOWARD SHOULDERS AND CHIN IS TUCKED TO CHEST WITH KNEES BENT.
3. PUT HANDS ON MAT AS BODY ROLLS TO SHOULDERS. HIPS ARE OFF MAT WITH LEGS TUCKED AND THIGHS CLOSE TO BODY.
4. EXTEND TOES TOWARD MAT OVERHEAD. KEEP HIPS LOW.
5. WHEN FEET CONTACT MAT, PUSH HARD WITH ARMS TO CLEAR HEAD FROM MAT.
6. END IN SQUAT WITH ARMS FORWARD.

Backward Straddle Roll

Start in a straddle stand position. Reach hands back between your legs to the mat. Thumbs are close beside the index fingers with palms back and fingers pointing forward on the mat.

Press hips backward. Roll inside of the fingers down to the palm. Keep weight on your arms with your thighs close to the chest.

Lift your feet as the buttocks touch the mat. Transfer your weight to the body. Round the back and tuck your chin to the chest.

Continue to roll backward. Lift your hands and place them by your ears with back of the hands toward the shoulders. Legs are straight and straddled with the toes pointed.

Roll onto the upper back. Hands are on the mat. Feet reach for the mat in line with your ears.

Push hard with your arms. Press the hips backward and straighten the elbows to clear your head from mat.

End in a straddle stand with head up and hands on the mat.

1. START IN STRADDLE STAND.
2. REACH HANDS BACK BETWEEN LEGS TO MAT. THUMBS ARE AGAINST INDEX FINGERS WITH PALMS BACKWARD AND FINGERS ON MAT POINTING TOWARD FACE.
3. PRESS HIPS BACKWARD. ROLL FINGERS DOWN TO PALMS. WEIGHT IS ON ARMS. THIGHS ARE CLOSE TO CHEST.
4. LIFT FEET AS BUTTOCKS TOUCH MAT. SHIFT WEIGHT TO BODY. TUCK CHIN AND ROUND BACK.
5. ROLL BACKWARD, LIFTING HANDS TO EARS AND BACK OF HANDS TO SHOULDERS. LEGS ARE STRADDLED AND STRAIGHT WITH TOES POINTED.
6. ROLL ON UPPER BACK. HANDS ARE ON MAT. FEET REACH MAT STRADDLED AND IN LINE WITH EARS.
7. ARMS PUSH HARD. PRESS HIPS BACKWARD. STRAIGHTEN ARMS TO CLEAR HEAD FROM MAT.
8. END IN STRADDLE STAND WITH HEAD UP AND HANDS ON MAT.

Forward Straddle Roll

Start in a straddle stand with your hands on the mat in front of shoulders.

Lean forward, shifting your weight onto the arms. Tuck the chin to your chest. Rise onto the balls of your feet.

Bend the elbows and roll forward. When on low back, hold straddled legs close to your chest. Keep a tight pike and reach your hands between your legs for the mat.

Lean forward and place hands on mat. Put outside edges of feet on the mat with your legs turned out at the hips.

Roll from the heels of the hands up to the palms and then onto the fingers. Push off the hands. Shift your weight forward. Lean forward.

End in a straddle stand with your hands on the mat in front of your body.

1. START IN STRADDLE STAND. HANDS ON MAT IN FRONT OF SHOULDERS.
2. LEAN FORWARD—SHIFT WEIGHT TO ARMS, TUCK CHIN AND RISE ONTO BALLS OF FEET.
3. BEND ELBOWS THEN ROLL FORWARD.
4. WHEN ON LOW BACK, HOLD STRADDLED LEGS CLOSE TO CHEST. KEEP PIKED AT HIPS. REACH HANDS FOR MAT BETWEEN LEGS.
5. LEAN FORWARD TO PLACE HANDS ON MAT.
6. PUT OUTSIDE EDGES OF FEET ON MAT. LEGS ARE TURNED OUT AT HIP.
7. ROLL FROM HEELS OF HANDS, UP PALMS AND ONTO FINGERS. PUSH OFF HANDS AND SHIFT WEIGHT FORWARD. LEAN FORWARD.
8. END IN STRADDLE STAND WITH HANDS ON MAT IN FRONT OF BODY.

Cartwheel

Start in a side stand with arms obliquely upward. Weight is on the right leg with the left leg to the side and toes pointed.

Shift weight onto your left leg. Bend the left leg and body to the left. Place your left hand on the mat and kick your right leg vertically.

Place your right hand on the mat then push the left leg off the mat. Head is positioned between your arms facing the mat. Back is straight and legs are straddled.

Do not stop upside down. Shift your weight from the left to right arm. Push off the left hand as the right leg reaches toward the mat. Keep the body stretched while placing your right foot on the mat.

Shift your weight to the right leg while pushing off the left hand. Put your left foot down and push off the right arm.

This movement constitutes an even four-count rhythm—1-2-3-4, or hand-hand-foot-foot.

End in side stand with feet slightly apart and arms obliquely upward.

1. **START IN SIDE STAND—WEIGHT ON RIGHT LEG, LEFT LEG TO SIDE WITH TOES POINTED AND ARMS OBLIQUELY UPWARD.**
2. **SHIFT WEIGHT TO LEFT LEG. BEND LEFT LEG AND BODY TO LEFT.**

3. PLACE LEFT HAND ON MAT. KICK RIGHT LEG TOWARD THE VERTICAL.

4. PLACE RIGHT HAND ON MAT. PUSH LEFT LEG OFF MAT. LEGS ARE STRADDLED WITH BACK STRAIGHT AND HEAD BETWEEN ARMS LOOKING AT MAT.

5. DO NOT STOP UPSIDE DOWN. SHIFT WEIGHT FROM LEFT TO RIGHT ARM.

6. PUSH OFF LEFT HAND AS RIGHT LEG REACHES TOWARD MAT. KEEP BODY STRETCHED.

7. PUT RIGHT FOOT ON MAT, SHIFT WEIGHT TO RIGHT LEG AND PUSH OFF LEFT HAND.

8. PUT LEFT FOOT DOWN THEN PUSH OFF RIGHT ARM.

9. MOVEMENT IS AN EVEN FOUR-COUNT, 1-2-3-4, HAND-HAND-FOOT-FOOT.

10. END IN SIDE STAND—FEET SLIGHTLY APART AND ARMS OBLIQUELY UPWARD.

Handstand Forward Roll

Start in a stand on the straight left leg with the right leg lifted in back, toes pointed and arms held vertically, a shoulder's-width apart.

Bend forward at the left hip, raising the right leg higher. Place hands on mat directly under your shoulders. Eyes are looking at your hands.

Push off the left leg as your right leg reaches the vertical. Join the legs at the vertical. The back and arms are straight.

Lean your body forward just past the vertical. Bend your elbows. Tuck chin to chest as your body lowers toward the mat. Pike at hips when the top of the shoulders touches the mat. Squeeze your legs tightly and control the hips.

Round the back and continue to roll forward. Bend the right knee as your buttocks contact the mat. Reach your arms forward.

End in a sit with right knee bent and left leg straight. Arms are forward.

1. STAND ON STRAIGHT LEFT LEG. BEND FORWARD AT LEFT HIP AND RAISE RIGHT LEG HIGHER.
2. PLACE HANDS ON MAT DIRECTLY UNDER SHOULDERS. FACE IS TOWARD HANDS.
3. PUSH OFF LEFT LEG AS RIGHT LEG REACHES THE VERTICAL.
4. JOIN LEGS TIGHTLY AT THE VERTICAL. BACK AND ARMS ARE STRAIGHT.
5. LEAN BODY JUST PAST THE VERTICAL.
6. BEND ELBOWS. TUCK CHIN TO CHEST AS BODY LOWERS TO MAT.
7. PIKE HIPS WHEN TOPS OF SHOULDERS TOUCH MAT. SQUEEZE LEGS TIGHTLY TO CONTROL HIPS.
8. ROUND BACK AND ROLL FORWARD.
9. AS HIPS TOUCH MAT, REACH HANDS FORWARD BEND RIGHT KNEE.
10. END SITTING POSITION, WITH RIGHT KNEE BENT AND LEFT LEG STRAIGHT. ARMS ARE FORWARD.

Cartwheel Twist to Split

Start in a side stand on the right leg with the left leg pointed out to the side. Arms are held obliquely upward.

Bend to the left side, while bending the left knee. Reach for the mat with the left hand.

Place your left hand on mat. Kick the right leg up to the vertical. Push off with the left leg. Place your right hand on the mat with fingers pointing away from your body. Face is directed at the mat between hands.

At the top of the cartwheel, swing the right leg toward the left hand. Keep the legs apart.

Rotate the left leg backward to a split position. Drop the body toward the mat in front of the hands. Shif your weight to the right arm.

Lift the left hand just before legs hit the mat so your body will be straight. Land in a split position with your right leg in front and body close to the right hand.

In the split with your right leg in front, the right arm is straight with your hand on the mat. Your left arm is straight and in a vertical position. Your head is up.

1. START IN SIDE STAND ON RIGHT LEG. LEFT LEG POINTS OUT TO SIDE. ARMS ARE OBLIQUELY UPWARD.
2. BEND LEFT KNEE AND BODY TO LEFT. REACH LEFT HAND FOR MAT.
3. PLACE LEFT HAND ON MAT.

4. KICK RIGHT LEG TO VERTICAL. PUT RIGHT HAND ON MAT, FINGERS POINTING AWAY FROM BODY. HEAD IS DOWN.

5. PUSH OFF LEFT LEG.

6. AT TOP OF CARTWHEEL POSITION, SWING RIGHT LEG TOWARD LEFT HAND. KEEP LEGS APART.

7. ROTATE LEFT LEG BACKWARD TO SPLIT POSITION.

8. DROP BODY TOWARD MAT IN FRONT OF HANDS. SHIFT WEIGHT TO RIGHT ARM.

9. LIFT LEFT HAND JUST BEFORE LEGS HIT MAT SO BODY IS STRAIGHT.

10. LAND IN SPLIT POSITION WITH RIGHT LEG FORWARD AND BODY CLOSE TO RIGHT HAND.

11. END IN SPLIT—RIGHT LEG IN FRONT, RIGHT ARM STRAIGHT WITH HAND ON MAT AND LEFT ARM STRAIGHT IN LINE WITH THE VERTICAL. HEAD IS UP.

Round-Off

Start with a run and a hurdle (straight leg hurdle is preferred). Arms are extended upward.

Put left leg in front and bend it. Reach for mat with left hand while keeping your elbow straight.

Kick your right leg upward to the vertical. Put the right hand on the mat and push off with the left leg as in a cartwheel. Join legs at the vertical. Twist your hips one quarter-turn inward. Pike at your hips and pull your legs downward. Push off strongly from the arms. Your body is momentarily suspended in air.

Lift the upper body and arms before feet land on the mat.

End in an upright stand. Knees and ankles are slightly bent. Back is straight with your head directed forward. Arms are up.

1. **START WITH RUN AND HURDLE. ARMS ARE UP.**
2. **PUT LEFT LEG IN FRONT THEN BEND IT AT THE KNEE. REACH LEFT HAND FOR MAT KEEPING ELBOW STRAIGHT.**
3. **KICK RIGHT LEG UP TO THE VERTICAL. PUT RIGHT HAND ON MAT.**
4. **PUSH OFF LEFT LEG, AS IN CARTWHEEL.**
5. **JOIN LEGS AT THE VERTICAL.**

6. TWIST HIPS ONE QUARTER-TURN INWARD.
7. PIKE HIPS AND PULL LEGS DOWNWARD.
8. PUSH STRONGLY OFF ARMS. BODY IS MOMENTARILY AIRBORNE.
9. LIFT UPPER BODY AND ARMS BEFORE FEET HIT MAT.
10. END UPRIGHT IN STAND WITH KNEES AND ANKLES BENT, BACK STRAIGHT, HEAD UP AND ARMS UP.

Front Handspring

Start with a run and a hurdle. Arms stretch upward. Put your left foot on the mat in front of your body. Reach for the mat with both hands. Elbows are straight. Body is straight as possible.

Kick the right leg upward as your body leans down. Thrust off the left leg, and kick it toward the right leg.

Join both legs at the vertical. Push hard off the hands to continue your legs overhead and toward the mat.

The body is airborne in a layout position with your head back. Legs are held tightly together, while the arms are in position near your head.

Rotate your body forward to raise the upper body. Land on your feet with your body stretched upward. Bend at the knees slightly to absorb the shock of landing.

End in stand with knees bent, arms up in front and head in normal position.

1. START WITH RUN AND HURDLE. ARMS STRETCH UPWARD.
2. PUT LEFT FOOT ON MAT IN FRONT OF BODY.
3. REACH HANDS FOR MAT WITH ELBOWS STRAIGHT AS POSSIBLE.
4. KICK RIGHT LEG UP AND IN BACK AS BODY LEANS FORWARD.
5. PLACE HANDS ON MAT. HEAD FACES MAT BETWEEN HANDS.

6. THRUST OFF LEFT LEG AND KICK IT TOWARD RIGHT LEG.

7. JOIN LEGS AT THE VERTICAL. PUSH STRONGLY OFF HANDS TO CONTINUE LEGS OVERHEAD TO MAT.

8. BODY IN LAYOUT POSITION IN AIR WITH HEAD BACK, LEGS TIGHT TOGETHER, ARMS NEAR HEAD.

9. ROTATE BODY FORWARD TO RAISE UPPER BODY TO VERTICAL.

10. LAND ON FEET—BODY STRETCHED UPWARD; KNEES BENT TO ABSORB FORCE OF LANDING.

11. END STANDING WITH KNEES BENT, ARMS UP IN FRONT, HEAD IN NEUTRAL POSITION. THIS STUNT IS ONE CONTINUOUS ACTION WITH NO PAUSES IN ANY POSITION.

flexibility movements

Flexibility movements are programmed to show flexibility and to give a change of pace from the stunts. They can be transitions or moves.

Front Limber (Limbre)

Start in a stand on the right leg with the left leg pointed in front. Arms are a shoulder's-width apart in front.

Step forward onto the straight left leg. Lift a straightened right leg up in back as the body leans forward from the left hip. Place both hands on the mat.

Push off your left leg. Join both the legs at the vertical. Body is stretched upward with your head facing the mat in front of the hands.

Keep the shoulders over your hands. Lower the legs overhead by arching at the low back. The back of your head is toward the buttocks.

Land on the balls of your feet and on the mat with your toes straight ahead. Push off your hands, keeping arms and head back. Tighten legs, then knees, thighs and hips. Push your hips slightly forward to bring the upper body up and forward.

End in a stand with your heels down on the mat, and the body stretched upward. Arms are vertical near the front of your face.

This is a continuous movement. Maintain control of your legs as they are lowered overhead to the mat.

1. **STAND ON RIGHT LEG, LEFT LEG POINTED IN FRONT. ARMS SHOULDER'S-WIDTH APART IN FRONT.**
2. **STEP FORWARD ONTO STRAIGHT LEFT LEG. LIFT STRAIGHT RIGHT LEG UP IN BACK. LEAN BODY FORWARD AT LEFT HIP.**
3. **PLACE HANDS ON MAT. PUSH OFF LEFT LEG.**
4. **JOIN LEGS AT THE VERTICAL. BODY STRETCHES UPWARD, HEAD LOOKING AT MAT IN FRONT OF HANDS.**
5. **KEEP SHOULDERS OVER HANDS. LOWER LEGS OVER HEAD BY ARCHING AT LOW BACK.**
6. **LAND ON BALLS OF FEET, TOES STRAIGHT AHEAD.**
7. **PUSH OFF HANDS. KEEP ARMS AND HEAD BACK. TIGHTEN LEGS STARTING AT LOWER LEG AND PROGRESSING UPWARD TO HIPS.**
8. **BRING UPPER BODY UP AND FORWARD.**

9. END STANDING WITH HEELS DOWN ON MAT AND BODY STRETCHED UPWARD. ARMS ARE HELD VERTICALLY IN FRONT OF FACE.

10. THIS IS A CONTINUOUS MOVEMENT. MAINTAIN CONTROL OF LEGS AS THEY LOWER OVERHEAD TO MAT.

Back Walkover

Start in a stand on the right leg with the left leg pointed in front. Arms are up in front, a shoulder's-width apart.

Lean arms, head, and upper body backward, lifting your left leg off the mat toward vertical.

Place your hands on the mat. Push hard off the right leg. Legs are in a split position. Head is pulled back toward your buttocks. Keep the body stretched.

Rotate the left leg toward the mat, keeping your legs in a split position. Place the left foot on the mat. Push off your hands and lower the right leg as the upper body is raised to the vertical.

End in a stand on the left leg with the right leg pointed behind. Arms are held vertically with your head facing forward.

1. STAND ON RIGHT LEG, LEFT LEG POINTED IN FRONT. ARMS UP ARE IN FRONT, A SHOULDER'S-WIDTH APART.
2. LEAN ARMS, HEAD AND UPPER BODY BACKWARD. LIFT LEFT LEG TOWARD THE VERTICAL.
3. PLACE HANDS ON MAT. PUSH HARD OFF LEFT LEG. LEGS IN SPLIT POSITION WITH HEAD PULLED TOWARD BUTTOCKS AND BODY STRETCHED.
4. ROTATE LEFT LEG TOWARD MAT. KEEP SPLIT POSITION.

5. PLACE LEFT FOOT ON MAT, PUSH OFF HANDS
AND LOWER RIGHT LEG AS YOU RAISE
UPPER BODY TO THE VERTICAL.

6. END STANDING ON LEFT LEG WITH RIGHT LEG
POINTED BEHIND, ARMS HELD VERTICALLY
AND HEAD LOOKING FORWARD.

Front Walkover

Start in stand on the left leg with the right leg
pointed behind. Arms are held upward in front, a
shoulder's-width apart.

Lift the right leg up in back as body leans forward
from the hip. Place your hands on the mat. Look
at mat in front of your hands. Push off the left leg.
Legs are in a split position.

Keep your body stretched while rotating the right
leg overhead toward the mat. Keep the split position on legs.

Place your right foot on the mat. Push off your
hands, keeping arms and head back. Hold the left
leg up in front. Push the hip and thigh of the right
leg forward to shift your weight forward. Lift your
upper body to the vertical as you lower the left leg.

End in a stand on the right leg with the left leg
pointed in front. Arms are up near front of face.
Head is in neutral position.

1. STAND ON LEFT LEG, RIGHT LEG POINTED
BEHIND AND ARMS UP IN FRONT, A
SHOULDER'S-WIDTH APART.

2. LIFT RIGHT LEG UP IN BACK. LEAN BODY
FORWARD FROM LEFT HIP.

3. PLACE HANDS ON MAT AND LOOK AT MAT IN
FRONT OF HANDS.

4. PUSH OFF LEFT LEG. LEGS ARE IN SPLIT
POSITION.

5. STRETCH BODY; ROTATE RIGHT LEG
OVERHEAD TOWARD MAT WHILE KEEPING
LEGS IN SPLIT POSITION.

6. PLACE RIGHT FOOT ON MAT. PUSH OFF
HANDS. KEEP ARMS AND HEAD BACK. HOLD
LEFT LEG UP IN FRONT.

7. PUSH HIP AND THIGH OFF LEFT LEG TO SHIFT WEIGHT FORWARD. LIFT UPPER BODY TO THE VERTICAL AS LEFT LEG LOWERS.
8. END STANDING ON RIGHT LEG WITH LEFT LEG POINTED IN FRONT. HEAD IS IN NEUTRAL POSITION WITH ARMS UP NEAR FRONT OF FACE.

positions

Positions may be momentarily held or moved right through. They can be of a high or low level.

Split

Start in a stand with the right leg in front of the left.

Lower your body to the mat, keeping your weight on the right leg, left leg or both legs. Move your legs away from each other—one forward, one backward.

End in a split position with the right leg in front. Left leg is behind with the knee turned out. The entire back of the right leg should touch the mat. Legs are straight with the toes pointed. Right arm is held obliquely upward with the left arm parallel to the left leg. Head is back, looking out over your left arm.

1. STAND WITH RIGHT LEG IN FRONT OF LEFT.
2. LOWER BODY TO MAT. WEIGHT ON EITHER OR BOTH FEET. LEGS MOVE AWAY FROM EACH OTHER, FORWARD AND BACKWARD.
3. END IN SPLIT POSITION, RIGHT LEG FORWARD, LEFT BACK WITH LEFT LEG TURNED OUT FROM HIP. LEGS ARE STRAIGHT AND TOES POINTED. RIGHT ARM HELD OBLIQUELY UPWARD. LEFT ARM IS PARALLEL TO LEFT LEG. BODY TWISTED SLIGHTLY TO LEFT. HEAD IS LOOKING OUT OVER LEFT ARM.

V Sit (Seat)

Start in a sitting position with your hands on mat behind the body. Fingers point away from body with elbows straight.

Lift straight legs up, keeping your back straight. Head is up with weight on the arms.

End in a piked or "V" position. Legs are straight and toes are pointed. Head is up.

1. SIT WITH HANDS ON MAT BEHIND BODY, ELBOWS ARE STRAIGHT AND FINGERS POINTED AWAY FROM BODY.
2. LIFT STRAIGHT LEGS UP; WEIGHT IS ON ARMS AND BACK IS STRAIGHT.
3. END IN "V" OR PIKED POSITION. LEGS ARE STRAIGHT WITH TOES POINTED, BACK STRAIGHT AND HEAD UP.

Deep Scale

Start in a stand on the right leg with the left leg pointed behind. Arms are up in front.

Lift the left leg upward in back. Lower the body forward while bending at the right hip.

End with the legs in a split position. Left leg is held high in back. Body is stretched forward in a low oblique position. Arms are in a low forward oblique position with the head up.

1. STAND ON RIGHT LEG, LEFT LEG POINTED BEHIND. ARMS ARE UP IN FRONT.
2. LIFT LEFT LEG UP IN BACK AND LOWER BODY FORWARD FROM RIGHT HIP.
3. END IN SPLIT POSITION STANDING ON RIGHT LEG WITH LEFT LEG HIGH IN BACK. BODY IS STRETCHED FORWARD IN A LOW OBLIQUE POSITION. ARMS ARE IN A LOW OBLIQUE FORWARD WITH HEAD UP.

Moderate Arabesque

Start in a stand on the right leg with a straight left leg pointed behind. Arms are crossed at the forearms in front of the chest with your left arm nearest the body. Palms face down.

Lift left leg upward in back to conclude just below the horizontal. Rise onto the ball of the right foot.

End high on ball of the right foot. Left leg is in an oblique position behind. Arms are crossed with palms facing in. Left arm is nearest body.

1. STAND ON RIGHT LEG WITH STRAIGHT LEFT LEG POINTED BEHIND. ARMS CROSSED AT FOREARMS IN FRONT OF CHEST, LEFT ARM NEAREST BODY. PALMS FACE BODY.
2. LIFT LEFT LEG UP IN BACK JUST BELOW THE HORIZONTAL.
3. RISE ONTO BALL OF RIGHT FOOT.
4. END HIGH ON BALL OF RIGHT FOOT WITH LEFT LEG HELD OBLIQUELY BEHIND. ARMS ARE CROSSED WITH LEFT ARM NEAREST CHEST WHILE PALMS FACE BODY. HEAD IS UP.

Back Attitude

Start by standing on the right leg with the left leg pointed behind. Right arm is held vertically with the left arm forward at the horizontal.

Lift the turned-out left leg in back. Bend the left knee and press your heel down so that the lower leg is parallel to the mat. Keep your knee lifted so it doesn't point downward. Your thigh is parallel to mat.

Rise onto the ball of the right foot. Head faces out over the left arm.

End up on the ball of the right foot. Left leg is bent behind and parallel to the mat with toes pointed. Right arm is held vertically and left arm horizontally in front.

1. STAND ON RIGHT LEG, LEFT LEG POINTED BEHIND. RIGHT ARM IS IN A VERTICAL POSITION. LEFT ARM IS FORWARD AT THE HORIZONTAL.
2. LIFT TURNED-OUT LEFT LEG IN BACK. BEND KNEE AND PRESS HEEL DOWN SO LEG IS PARALLEL TO MAT. KNEE SHOULD NOT POINT DOWNWARD.
3. RISE ONTO BALL OF RIGHT FOOT. LOOK OUT OVER LEFT ARM.
4. END HIGH ON BALL OF RIGHT FOOT, LEFT LEG BENT BEHIND AND PARALLEL TO MAT. TOES ARE POINTED. RIGHT ARM IS HELD VERTICALLY AND LEFT ARM HORIZONTALLY FORWARD. LOOK OUT OVER LEFT ARM.

rules simplified

Dimensions

The floor exercise area is 12 meters x 12 meters or 39.37 feet x 39.37 feet. The surface is usually matted or covered by a carpetlike material. A white line usually marks the area with a foot or more of extra area along the edges.

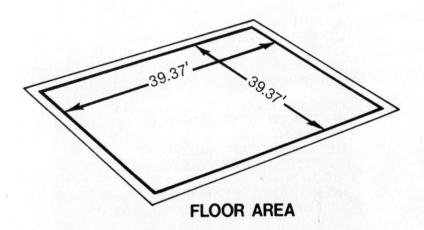

FLOOR AREA

Floor exercise is a combination of dance, flexibility or acrobatic movements, and tumbling stunts performed to music. The time limit is one minute to one minute and thirty seconds. A warning signal is given at one minute and twenty-five seconds.

Compositionally a *floor exercise routine* must contain the following parts: Acrobatic elements, tumbling passes, dance elements: turns, leaps, poses, locomotor patterns, floor movements and body movements of various types.

There should be changes in levels and rhythm with dynamic and soft parts. Interesting floor patterns and directional changes should be incorporated in the routine also.

Music is an important consideration when composing a floor exercise routine. It should have tempo changes and be suitable to the gymnast's level of execution, morphology and temperament. It must be played on a single instrument with the piano usually preferred.

Evaluation of an optional floor exercise routine is as follows:

DIFFICULTY	4.0 points
ORIGINALITY AND VALUE OF COMBINATIONS . .	1.5
GENERAL COMPOSITION	.5
EXECUTION	1.5
AMPLITUDE	1.5
GENERAL IMPRESSION	1.0
	10.0 points

SPECIFIC PENALTIES: DEDUCTIONS

FALL ON FLOOR	−1.0
REPETITION OF MISSED ELEMENT	−0.5
MUSICAL ACCOMPANIMENT NOT ACCORDING TO REGULATION	−1.0
NO HARMONY BETWEEN END OF EXERCISE AND MUSIC . .	−0.5

The rules and notes about each section were based on the following: *1970 Code of Points for Women —International Gymnastics Federation; June 1971-June 1973, Gymnastics Guide*—The Division for Girls' and Women's Sports.

For complete rules information, consult these sources:

Division for Girls'
 and Women's Sports
1201 Sixteenth St., N.W.
Washington, D.C. 20036

F.I.G. Code of Points for Women
U.S. Gymnastics Federation
P.O. Box 4699
Tucson, Arizona 85717

vaulting

Vaulting consists of a run or approach, hurdle, takeoff, pre-flight, body of the vault, post-flight and landing. Each part is dependent upon the part preceding. Therefore, it all starts with a good run.

The approach, hurdle, and takeoff remain almost the same for every vault. The body position during pre-flight may change. The body of the vault may be changed. Landing technique is the same for any vault, but the body direction may change.

Body control is an important factor while vaulting. The legs should be tight and straight (except in squat-type vaults). Arms should not reach behind the head, and the back should not arch.

A vaulter knows when she has **really** vaulted as well as when she has merely **"flown"** between the board and the horse.

preparation

Approach or Run

The run or approach starts from sixty or eighty feet from the reuther board. It is a run which resembles a sprint. The arms move forward and backward, not side to side. The body leans slightly forward. Keep the center of gravity as high as possible. The run should be smooth and even, so as to prevent bouncing up and down. The run should build speed with the last three to five steps at a constant speed.

1. START SIXTY TO EIGHTY FEET FROM REUTHER BOARD.
2. SPRINT TO BUILD SPEED.
3. ARMS MOVE FORWARD AND BACKWARD, NOT SIDE TO SIDE.
4. BODY LEANS SLIGHTLY FORWARD. KEEP CENTER OF GRAVITY HIGH.
5. LAST THREE TO FIVE STEPS ACHIEVE CONSTANT SPEED.

Hurdle

The hurdle begins with the last step of the approach. Three to five steps in front of the reuther board, take off from one foot. Quickly and forcefully swing the other leg in front. The arms are in back. Join the legs together.

This hurdle is long and low. Keep the feet close to the floor. The knees should not lift high in front.

Land on both feet slightly more than halfway up on the board. The knees and ankles bend slightly. The arms swing to a low position in front of the body.

1. BEGIN WITH LAST STEP OF APPROACH.
2. THREE TO FIVE STEPS IN FRONT OF BOARD TAKE OFF ON ONE FOOT.
3. QUICKLY AND FORCEFULLY SWING OTHER LEG IN FRONT WITH ARMS HELD BACK.
4. JOIN LEGS TOGETHER.
5. KEEP FEET CLOSE TO FLOOR. HURDLE LONG AND LOW. DO NOT LIFT KNEES HIGH IN FRONT.
6. LAND ON BOTH FEET, HEELS BARELY TOUCHING BOARD, SLIGHTLY MORE THAN HALFWAY UP ON BOARD.
7. LEGS ARE TIGHT WITH KNEES AND ANKLES SLIGHTLY BENT. ARMS ARE DOWN IN FRONT OF BODY.

Takeoff

To *take off* very quickly drive or "punch" off the board. Punch by explosively pushing off the toes and balls of your feet. Knees and ankles are straightened.

Thrust the arms forward and upward to an oblique position in front of your face, halfway between the horizontal and vertical.

1. FROM THE HURDLE, QUICKLY "PUNCH" OFF BOARD. PUSH OFF BALLS OF FEET AND TOES. STRAIGHTEN KNEES AND ANKLES.

2. THRUST ARMS FORWARD AND UPWARD TO OBLIQUE POSITION IN FRONT OF FACE.

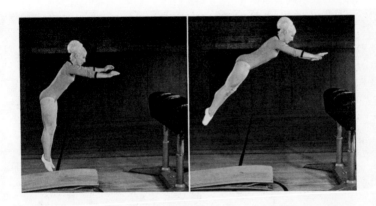

3. GOOD RUN AND TAKEOFF IMPORTANT TO SUCCESSFUL VAULT.

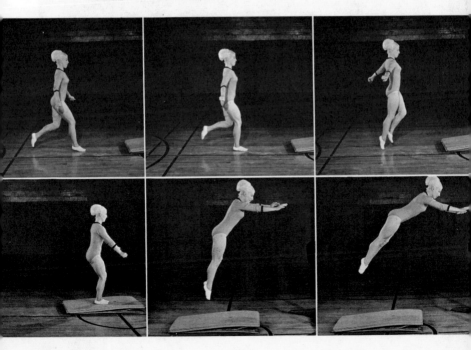

pre-flight
body position

Bent Hip

From the takeoff, the body lifts upward due to the change of momentum upward (from forward) in the takeoff. Hold your breath to aid the tightness and control of your body.

At height of flight, the hips are bent.

Place your hands a shoulder's-width apart on top of the horse after your body has reached the highest point in pre-flight. Fingers point forward. Do not support your weight on the hands to attain body position.

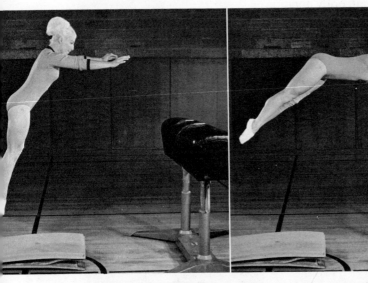

1. **BODY LIFTS UPWARD FROM TAKEOFF DUE TO CHANGE OF MOMENTUM IN TAKEOFF.**

2. **HOLD BREATH TO AID BODY CONTROL.**

3. **BEND HIPS AT HEIGHT OF FLIGHT.**

4. **AT HIGHEST POINT OF PRE-FLIGHT PLACE HANDS SHOULDER'S-WIDTH APART ON TOP OF HORSE. FINGERS POINT FORWARD. DO NOT SUPPORT BODY WEIGHT ON HANDS TO ATTAIN BODY POSITION.**

Horizontal Straight Body

From the takeoff, the body lifts upward due to the change of momentum from forward to upward. Continue to hold your breath to aid body tightness and control.

At the height of flight, the hips are straight and the body is stretched horizontally to the floor.

Place your hands on top of the horse, a shoulder's-width apart after your body has reached the highest point of pre-flight. Fingers are pointed forward. Do not support your body weight on the hands to attain body position.

1. BODY LIFTS UPWARD FROM TAKEOFF DUE TO CHANGE OF MOMENTUM IN TAKEOFF.
2. HOLD BREATH TO AID BODY CONTROL.
3. HIPS ARE STRAIGHT AT HEIGHT OF FLIGHT, BODY STRETCHED HORIZONTALLY TO FLOOR.
4. PLACE HANDS ON TOP OF HORSE, A SHOULDER'S-WIDTH APART, AT HIGHEST POINT IN PRE-FLIGHT, FINGERS POINTING FORWARD. DO NOT SUPPORT BODY WEIGHT ON HANDS TO ATTAIN BODY POSITION.

vaults

Squat Vault

As your hands reach the top of the horse at the highest point in pre-flight, bend at the hips. Tightly tuck the knees to your chest.

Push hands forward and upward off the horse as your body reaches the top of horse. Look forward while your body continues over the horse.

Stretch your body to an open position while in air.

Land on the balls of your feet. Bend the knees and ankles to absorb the force of landing. Press heels into the mat to maintain balance. Arms are held obliquely upward in front of your face.

End in a stand with arms at your sides.

This vault may be done from a bent-hip or horizontal-straight-body position during pre-flight.

1. **BEND HIPS AS HANDS REACH TOP OF HORSE AT HIGHEST POINT IN PRE-FLIGHT.**
2. **TUCK KNEES TIGHTLY TO CHEST.**

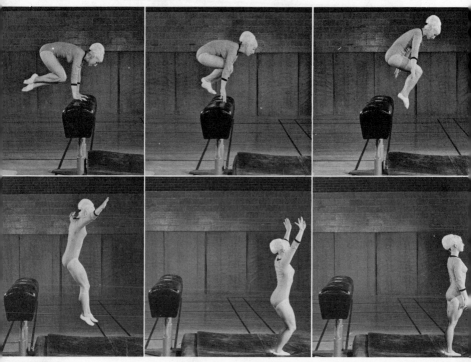

3. PUSH HANDS FORWARD AND UPWARD OFF HORSE AS BODY REACHES POSITION ABOVE TOP OF HORSE. LOOK FORWARD.

4. STRETCH BODY TO OPEN POSITION WHILE IN AIR.

5. LAND ON BALLS OF FEET. BEND KNEES AND ANKLES TO ABSORB FORCE OF LANDING. PRESS HEELS INTO MAT TO MAINTAIN BALANCE. ARMS HELD OBLIQUELY UPWARD IN FRONT OF FACE.

6. END IN STAND. ARMS AT SIDES.

7. THIS VAULT MAY BE DONE FROM BENT-HIP OR HORIZONTAL-STRAIGHT-BODY PRE-FLIGHT.

Flank Vault to Left

As your hands reach the top of the horse from pre-flight, lift the legs to the right side. Legs are held tightly together.

Lift your right hand to allow the legs to pass over the top of the horse followed by the left side of the body (flank).

As legs reach a position above the top of the horse, push off with your left hand, forward and upward as your body faces forward. Then stretch the body to an open position while in air.

Land on the balls of your feet. Face forward with your back to the horse. Knees and ankles bend to absorb the force of landing. Press heels into the mat to aid in maintaining your balance. Arms are held obliquely upward in front of your face.

End in stand with your back to the horse and arms at your sides.

This vault may be done from a bent-hip or horizontal-straight-body pre-flight. It may be done to either the right or left side.

1. LIFT LEGS TO RIGHT AS HANDS REACH TOP OF HORSE AT HEIGHT OF PRE-FLIGHT. LEGS HELD TIGHTLY TOGETHER.

2. LIFT RIGHT HAND TO ALLOW LEGS TO PASS OVER TOP OF HORSE. LEFT SIDE (FLANK) OF BODY ALSO PASSES OVER TOP OF HORSE.

3. PUSH OFF LEFT HAND AS LEGS REACH POSITION OVER TOP OF HORSE. BODY FACES FORWARD.
4. STRETCH BODY TO OPEN POSITION WHILE IN AIR.
5. LAND WITH BACK TO HORSE ON BALLS OF FEET. KNEES AND ANKLES BEND TO ABSORB FORCE OF LANDING. PRESS HEELS INTO MAT TO AID BALANCE. ARMS HELD OBLIQUELY UPWARD IN FRONT OF FACE.
6. END IN STAND. ARMS AT SIDES.
7. THIS VAULT MAY BE DONE FROM A BENT-HIP OR HORIZONTAL-STRAIGHT-BODY PRE-FLIGHT. IT MAY BE DONE TO RIGHT OR LEFT SIDE.

Rear Vault to Right

With your body facing forward in pre-flight, place both hands on top of the horse. Fingers point forward. Lift legs to the right and then lift your right hand off of the horse.

Turn the left hip so that the backs of your legs (rear position) pass over the top of the horse.

Push your left hand forward and upward off the

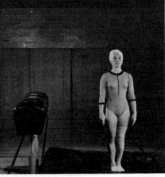

top of the horse. Reach with your right hand for the top of the horse as your body passes over the top then push your right hand off the horse.

Stretch your body to an open position in air.

Land with the right side to the horse. Bend knees and ankles to absorb the force of landing. **Press heels into the mat to aid balance.** Arms are held obliquely upward.

End in a stand with your right side to the horse and arms at your sides.

This vault may be done from a bent-hip or horizontal-straight-body pre-flight. It may be done to the right or left side.

1. **PLACE HANDS ON TOP OF HORSE. BODY FACES FORWARD IN PRE-FLIGHT WITH FINGERS POINTING FORWARD.**
2. **LIFT LEGS TO RIGHT.**
3. **LIFT RIGHT HAND OFF HORSE.**
4. **TURN LEFT HIP. BACKS OF LEGS (REAR POSITION) PASS OVER TOP OF HORSE.**
5. **PUSH LEFT HAND FORWARD AND UPWARD OFF HORSE.**

6. REACH RIGHT HAND FOR TOP OF HORSE AS BODY PASSES ABOVE TOP OF HORSE.
7. PUSH RIGHT HAND OFF FROM HORSE.
8. STRETCH BODY TO OPEN POSITION IN AIR.
9. LAND WITH RIGHT SIDE TO HORSE. BEND KNEES AND ANKLES TO ABSORB FORCE OF LANDING. PRESS HEELS INTO MAT TO MAINTAIN BALANCE. HOLD ARMS OBLIQUELY UPWARD.
10. END IN STAND—RIGHT SIDE TO HORSE AND ARMS AT SIDES. THIS VAULT MAY BE DONE FROM A BENT-HIP OR HORIZONTAL-STRAIGHT-BODY PRE-FLIGHT. IT MAY BE DONE TO THE RIGHT OR LEFT SIDE.

Stoop Vault

From pre-flight, place both hands on top of the horse, a shoulder's-width apart. Fingers point forward.

Pike hips. Keep legs straight and tightly together. Push hands forward and upward off the horse as feet start between your arms. Stretch body to an open position in air.

Land with your back to the horse. Bend knees and ankles to absorb the force of landing. Press heels into the mat to aid balance. Arms are held obliquely up in front of your face.

End in a stand with your back to the horse and arms down at your sides.

This vault may be done from a bent-hip or horizontal-straight-body pre-flight.

1. PLACE HANDS ON TOP OF HORSE, A SHOULDER'S-WIDTH APART. FINGERS POINT FORWARD.
2. PIKE HIPS.
3. KEEP LEGS STRAIGHT AND TIGHTLY TOGETHER.
4. PUSH HANDS FORWARD AND UPWARD OFF HORSE AS FEET START BETWEEN ARMS.
5. STRETCH BODY TO OPEN POSITION IN AIR.
6. LAND WITH BACK TO HORSE. BEND KNEES AND ANKLES TO ABSORB FORCE OF LANDING. PRESS HEELS INTO MAT TO AID BALANCE. ARMS ARE HELD OBLIQUELY UP IN FRONT OF FACE.

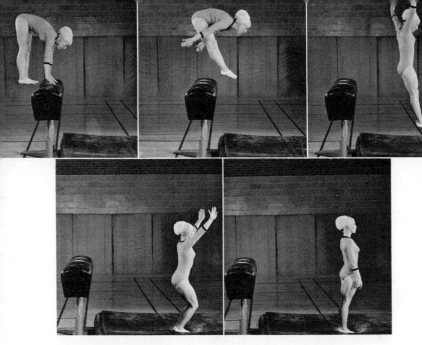

7. END IN STAND WITH BACK TO HORSE AND
ARMS DOWN AT SIDES. THIS VAULT MAY BE
DONE FROM A BENT-HIP OR HORIZONTAL-
STRAIGHT-BODY PRE-FLIGHT.

Straddle Vault

From the pre-flight, place your hands on top of
the horse. Fingers point forward. Open the legs
to a straddle position. Knees are straight.

Push the hands forward and upward off the horse
as the body passes above the top of the horse.

Pull the legs together as soon as they pass the
horse. Stretch the body to an open position in the
air.

Land with the feet together. Your back is to the
horse. Bend the knees and ankles to absorb the
force of landing. Press the heels into the mat to
aid balance. Arms are held obliquely forward and
upward in front of the face.

End in a stand with your back to the horse and arms
down at your sides.

This vault may be done from a bent-hip or horizontal-straight-body pre-flight.

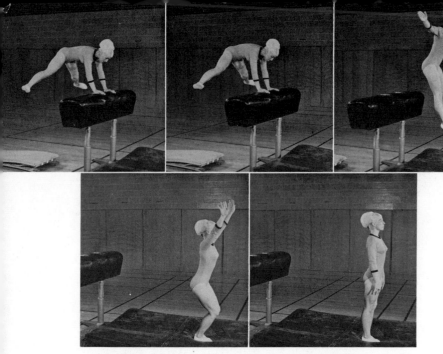

1. FROM PRE-FLIGHT, PLACE HANDS ON TOP OF HORSE. FINGERS POINT FORWARD.
2. OPEN LEGS TO STRADDLE POSITION. KNEES ARE STRAIGHT.
3. PUSH HANDS FORWARD AND UPWARD OFF HORSE AS BODY PASSES ABOVE TOP OF HORSE.
4. PULL LEGS TOGETHER WHEN PAST HORSE.
5. STRETCH BODY TO OPEN POSITION IN AIR.
6. LAND WITH FEET TOGETHER AND BACK TO HORSE. BEND KNEES AND ANKLES TO ABSORB FORCE OF LANDING. PRESS HEELS INTO MAT TO AID BALANCE. ARMS ARE HELD OBLIQUELY UPWARD IN FRONT OF FACE.
7. END IN STAND—BACK TO HORSE AND ARMS DOWN AT SIDES. THIS VAULT MAY BE DONE FROM BENT-HIP OR HORIZONTAL-STRAIGHT-BODY PRE-FLIGHT.

Headspring Vault

From the pre-flight, place your hands a shoulder's-width apart on top of the horse.

Pike the hips slightly as your hands contact the horse. Bend your elbows to lower the top of the head to the horse. Head is in line with your hands.

Keep the feet low. Push your hips overhead to an off-balance position.

When hips are off-balance over the head, push hard with your arms to straighten the elbows. Open the hips with an explosive action (kip), forcing the thighs away from the chest. Keep your head in a normal position.

Fly through air in a straight body or layout position. The back is only slightly arched. Arms are extended by the ears.

Land with your back to the horse. Bend knees and ankles to absorb the force of landing. Press heels into the mat to aid balance. Arms are held obliquely up in front of your face.

End in a stand with your arms down at sides.

1. **FROM PRE-FLIGHT, PLACE HANDS A SHOULDER'S-WIDTH APART ON TOP OF HORSE.**
2. **PIKE HIPS SLIGHTLY AS HANDS CONTACT HORSE. BEND ELBOWS TO LOWER TOP OF HEAD TO HORSE. HEAD IN LINE WITH HANDS.**
3. **KEEP FEET LOW. PUSH HIPS OVERHEAD TO OFF-BALANCE POSITION.**
4. **WITH HIPS OFF-BALANCE OVERHEAD, PUSH ARMS HARD TO STRAIGHTEN ELBOWS. OPEN HIPS WITH EXPLOSIVE ACTION. FORCE THIGHS AWAY FROM CHEST. KEEP HEAD IN NORMAL POSITION.**

5. FLY THROUGH AIR IN LAYOUT POSITION. BACK IS SLIGHTLY ARCHED, AND ARMS EXTENDED BY EARS.
6. LAND WITH BACK TO HORSE AND BODY ROTATED TO THE VERTICAL. BEND KNEES AND ANKLES TO ABSORB FORCE OF LANDING. PRESS HEELS INTO MAT TO AID BALANCE. ARMS ARE HELD OBLIQUELY UP IN FRONT OF FACE.
7. END IN STAND WITH ARMS DOWN AT SIDES. NOTE: THIS VAULT IS IN DISPUTE AS A COMPETITIVE VAULT, BUT IS USEFUL FOR CLASSWORK.

Dimensions

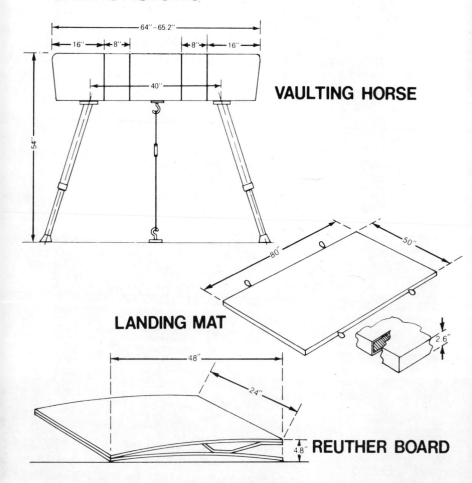

VAULTING HORSE

LANDING MAT

REUTHER BOARD

rules simplified

The **vaulting horse** is padded and covered with leather. In compulsory vaulting the gymnast is allowed two attempts. The better score of the two is the score which counts.

In optional vaulting, the gymnast is allowed two executions. She may do the same vault twice or do two different vaults. The better of the two scores is counted.

In compulsory vaulting, the vault is judged from ten points, regardless of the original point value of the vault.

Each optional vault has its own value. Vault values are listed in the FIG Women's Code of Points, Amateur Athletic Union of the United States, 3400 W. 86th St., Indianapolis, Indiana 46268.

Some Vault Values Are:

	BENT HIP	HORIZONTAL-STRAIGHT-BODY
Squat	5.0	6.5
Flank	5.0	—
Rear	5.0	—
Stoop	5.5	7.0
Straddle	5.5	7.0

Vaulting is Scored in Six Areas:

	Maximum Deduction
PRE-FLIGHT	2.0
PUSH OFF, REPULSION	2.0
OFF-FLIGHT, POST-FLIGHT	2.0
BODY POSITION AND STRETCH DURING POST-FLIGHT	2.0
DIRECTION OF VAULT	0.5
GENERAL BALANCE THROUGHOUT VAULT	1.5

Some Specific Deductions for Horizontal Vaults:

Maximum Deduction

STRADDLING LEGS TOO SOON
  (STRADDLE VAULT) . . . .   up to 0.5
TUCKING LEGS TOO SOON
  (SQUAT VAULT) . . . .   up to 0.5
BENDING LEGS
  (STOOP VAULT) . . . .   up to 1.0
TOUCHING HORSE WITH FEET   up to 0.5
OMISSION OF STRETCH OF
  BODY IN POST-FLIGHT 2.0

Other Specific Deductions for Vaulting:

LANDING ON FLOOR
  OUT OF BALANCE . . . .   up to 0.3
TOUCHING THE HANDS
  ON THE FLOOR 0.5
SUPPORTING THE HANDS
  ON THE FLOOR 1.0
FALL ON THE KNEES 1.5
FALL ON THE PELVIS 2.0
COACH BETWEEN THE
  BOARD AND HORSE 1.0
AID BY COACH
  DURING VAULT . . . .   vault is voided
AID BY COACH ON
  LANDING ON FLOOR 2.0

The approach and hurdle are not considered in the scoring of a vault.

For complete rules information, consult these sources:

Division for Girls'
  and Women's Sports
1201 Sixteenth St., N.W.
Washington, D.C. 20036

F.I.G. Code of Points for Women
U.S. Gymnastics Federation
P.O. Box 4699
Tucson, Arizona 85717

tips for beginning vaulting

1. Start vaulting onto stacked flat mats of various heights until they are built up to the height of the horse.

2. Begin vaulting with the board no closer than three feet from the horse. As you learn body control and can speed up the run, the board should be moved back a bit at a time. Continue to move board back from horse as you get stronger so that you can get good body stretch in the pre-flight. Eventually as an intermediate or advanced vaulter, you will use the board at a body's-length distance or more from the horse.

3. Learn from a bent-hip position and then progress to the horizontal-straight-body position. Practice stretching the body a little more each vault until a straight body is attained.

4. Pad the board with a thin mat or board cover to avoid sore legs when practicing.

5. Vaulting is an event which takes quick, explosive action of the legs and feet. Any activity which develops this action can be helpful.

6. Although vaulting is the shortest event in competition, it needs as much practice as the other events because it is one-quarter of the total all-around score.

glossary of gymnastics terms

AAU—Amateur Athletic Union of the United States.

Aerial—A stunt or dance move done in the air free of support.

All-Around—Women's four Olympic events: balance beam, floor exercise, uneven parallel bars and vaulting.

All-Around Champion—Highest scoring gymnast using the all-around events. Considered to be the best gymnast in that particular meet or competition.

Attitude—A leg position; a leg in front or behind the body. The knee is bent with the leg turned out parallel to the floor.

Compulsory Routine—A prescribed routine. Written in detail, it must be performed as written with certain exceptions.

DGWS—Division for Girls' and Women's Sports. A part of the American Association for Health, Physical Education and Recreation (AHPER).

FIG—International Gymnastic Federation. A governing body for international gymnastics.

Flip—A term used synonymously with somersault or salto meaning to turn over in the air.

Head Judge—Judge designated to be the head of the other judges on a particular event.

Inverted Support—A position of support upside down. Support may be on the hands or head.

IOC—International Olympic Committee. The governing body of the Olympic Games.

Kip—A movement or action where the body pikes and extends rapidly.

Lay Out—A body position. The body is extended in an almost straight line, the back is only very slightly arched.

Nationals—Term used to describe United States National Gymnastic Championships held once a year.

Oblique—A position of the arms in relation to the body. Usually halfway between the horizontal and vertical. It may be in front, behind or at the side of the body.

Optional Routine—A creative exercise or routine composed by the coach, the gymnast or both.

Pan Am's—Pan American Games. Competition between the American continents includes gymnastic events.

Pike—A body position in which the hips are bent so that the thighs are near the chest. Usually done with straight legs.

Punch—An explosive action off the feet or hands. Very quickly getting off the floor or apparatus. A short, powerful action.

Reuther board—A takeoff board which gets its spring by a slight flex in the wood. It is slightly inclined to aid in changing forward momentum to upward momentum.

Salto—A term for aerial somersault or flip. Used in European texts and getting more use in the United States. May be done forward, backward or sideward.

Scratch—To remove a name from the list of competitors in a meet.

Side Horse—Piece of equipment. Used by women for vaulting, it is used widthwise.

Specialist—A gymnast who concentrates on one or two events instead of going "all-around". A specialist usually may not compete in National Championships unless she competes all-around.

Stick—To land from a dismount or vault without loss of balance or movement of the feet.

Stoop—To pass the legs through the arms without bending the knees.

Straddle—A leg position. The legs are spread wide apart.

Superior Judge—In higher level competition, the fifth judge. She is usually more qualified than the other four judges and her score counts if there is a dispute.

Tour—To turn. May be done in air or on floor or on apparatus.

Tuck—A body position. Bend the knees to the chest, round the back and keep heels close to the buttocks.

USGF—United States Gymnastic Federation. A governing body for gymnastics in the United States.

USOC—United States Olympic Committee. The governing body for the Olympic Games in the United States.

World Games—Competition between the nations of the world. Held between the Olympic years.

notes

notes

notes

IMMANUEL LUTHERAN LIBRARY